Benny Goodman

The King of Swing

Filiquarian Publishing, LLC.

Filiquarian Publishing, LLC.

Benny Goodman

The King of Swing

Benny Goodman, born Benjamin David Goodman,[1] (May 30, 1909 – June 13, 1986) was an American jazz musician and clarinetist, known as "King of Swing", "Patriarch of the Clarinet", "The Professor", and "Swing's Senior Statesman".

Childhood and Early Years

Goodman was born in Chicago, the ninth of twelve children[2] of poor Jewish immigrants from Poland who lived in the Maxwell Street neighborhood. His father, David Goodman, was a tailor from Warsaw, his mother, Dora Rezinski, was from Kaunas. His parents met in Baltimore, Maryland and moved to Chicago before Benny was born.[3]

When Benny was 10, his father enrolled Benny and two older brothers in music lessons at the Kehelah Jacob Synagogue. The next year he joined the boys club band at Jane Addams's Hull House, where he received lessons from the director James Sylvester. Also important during this period were his two years of instruction from the classically trained clarinetist Franz Schoepp.[4]

His early influences were New Orleans jazz clarinetists working in Chicago, notably Johnny Dodds, Leon Roppolo, and Jimmy Noone.[5] Goodman learned quickly, becoming a strong player at an early age. He was soon playing professionally while still 'in short pants', playing clarinet in various bands.

When Goodman was 16, he joined one of Chicago's top bands, the Ben Pollack Orchestra, with which he made his first recordings in 1926.[6] He made his first record on Vocalion under his own name two years later. Remaining with Pollack through 1929, Goodman recorded with the regular Pollack band and smaller groups drawn from the orchestra. The side sessions produced scores of often hot sides recorded for the various dime-store record labels under ewildering array of group names, such as Mills' Musical Clowns, Goody's Good Timers, The Hotsy Totsy Gang, Jimmy Backen's Toe Ticklers, Dixie Daisies, and Kentucky Grasshoppers.

Goodman's father, David, was a working-class immigrant about whom Benny said (interview, 'Downbeat', Feb 8, 1956); "...Pop worked in the stockyards, shoveling lard in its unrefined state. He had those boots, and he'd come home at the end of the day exhausted, stinking to high heaven, and when he walked in it made me sick. I couldn't stand it. I couldn't stand the idea of Pop every day standing in that stuff, shoveling it around".

On December 9, 1929 David Goodman was killed in a traffic accident shortly after Benny joined the Pollack band and had urged his father to retire, now that he (Benny) and his brother (Harry) were doing well as professional musicians. According to James Lincoln Collier, "Pop looked Benny in the eye and said, 'Benny, you take care of yourself, I'll take care of myself.'" Collier continues: "It was an unhappy choice. Not long afterwards, as he was stepping down from a street car — according to one story — he was struck by a car. He never regained consciousness and died in the hospital the next day. It was itter blow to the family, and it haunted Benny to the end that his father had not lived to see the success he, and some of the others, made of themselves."[7] "Benny described his father's death as 'the saddest thing that ever happened in our family.'"[8]

Career

Goodman left for New York City and became a successful session musician during the late 1920s and early 1930s. He made a reputation as a solid player who was prepared and reliable. He played with the nationally known bands of Ben Selvin, Red Nichols, Isham Jones, and Ted Lewis. He also recorded musical soundtracks for movie shorts; some fans are convinced that Benny Goodman's clarinet can be heard on the soundtrack of One A. M., a Charlie Chaplin comedy re-released to theaters in 1934.

In 1934 Goodman auditioned for NBC's Let's Dance(sponsered by Ritz crackers), a well regarded radio program that featured various styles of dance music. Since he needed new arrangements every week for the show, his agent, John Hammond, suggested that he purchase jazz charts from Fletcher Henderson, an African-American musician from Atlanta who had New York's most popular African-American band in the 1920s and early 1930s.

Goodman, a wise businessman, caught Henderson in 1929 when the stock market crashed. He purchased all of Henderson's song books, and hired Henderson's band members to teach his musicians how to play the music.

The combination of Goodman's solid clarinet playing, the Henderson charts, and the well-rehearsed band made Goodman a rising star in the mid-1930s, earning him the title "King of Swing." In early 1935, Goodman and his band were one of three bands featured on Let's Dance. His radio broadcasts from New York aired too late to attract a large East Coast audience. However, unknown to him, the timeslot gave him an avid following on the West Coast. He and his band remained on Let's

Dance until May of that year when a strike forced the cancellation of the radio show.

With nothing else to do, the band set out on a tour of America. However, at a number of engagements the band received a hostile reception, as many in the audiences expected smoother, sweeter jazz as opposed to the "hot" style that Goodman's band was accustomed to playing. By August of 1935, Goodman found himself with and that was nearly broke, disillusioned and ready to quit. It was at this moment that everything for the band and jazz changed.

Palomar Ballroom Engagement

The last scheduled stop of the tour came on August 21, 1935 at the Palomar Ballroom in Los Angeles. Goodman and his band were scheduled for a three-week engagement. The Palomar provided the ideal environment, as there was a huge dance floor with a capacity of 4,000 couples. On hand for the engagement were famed musicians Gene Krupa, Bunny Berigan, and Helen Ward. The first night, Goodman and his band cautiously began playing recently purchased stock arrangements. The reaction was, at best, tepid. Seeing the reaction, Krupa said "If we're gonna die, Benny, let's die playing our own thing." [9] As George Spink states:

"At the beginning of the next set, Goodman told the band to put aside the stock arrangements and called for charts by Fletcher Henderson and other swing arrangers who were writing for the band. When trumpeter Bunny Berigan played his solos on Henderson's versions of "Sometimes I'm Happy" and "King Porter Stomp," the Palomar dancers cheered like crazy and exploded with applause! They gathered around the bandstand to listen to this new music." [9]

This was the music the enthusiastic audience had heard on the "Let's Dance" radio show and that they had come to hear.

Over the nights of the engagement, a new dance labeled the "Jitterbug" captured the dancers on the floor, and a new craze had begun.[10] Onlookers gathered around the edges of the ballroom floor. Within days of the opening, newspapers around the country were headlining stories about the new phenomenon that had started at the Palomar. Goodman was finally a nationally known star, and the Swing Eregan, led by Goodman. Following this the big band era exploded.

Carnegie Hall Concert

"In bringing jazz to Carnegie, [Benny Goodman was], in effect, smuggling American contraband into the halls of European high culture, and Goodman and his 15 men pull[ed] it off with the audacity and precision of Ocean's Eleven."[11]

In late 1937, Goodman's publicist Wynn Nathanson attempted a publicity stunt in the form of suggesting Goodman and his band should play Carnegie Hall in New York City. "Benny Goodman was initially hesitant about the concert, fearing for the worst; however, when his film Hollywood Hotel opened to rave reviews and giant lines, he threw himself into the work. He gave up several dates and insisted on holding rehearsals inside Carnegie Hall to familiarize the band with the lively acoustics."[12]

The concert was the evening of January 16, 1938. It sold out weeks before, with the capacity 2,760 seats going for the top price of US$2.75 a seat, for the time a very high price. The concert began with three contenporary numbers from the Goodman band—"Don't Be That Way", "Sometimes I'm Happy", and "One O'Clock Jump". Then came a history of jazz, starting with a Dixieland quartet performing "Sensation Rag". Once again, initial crowd reaction, though polite, was tepid. The came a jam session on "Honeysuckle Rose" featuring members of the Count Basie and Duke Ellington bands as guests. It did not go as well as hoped. As the concert went on, things livened up. The Goodman band and quartet took over the stage and performed the numbers that had already made them famous. Some of the later trio and quartet numbers were well-received, and a vocal on "Loch Lomond" by Martha Tilton, though nothing special, provoked five curtain calls and cries for an encore. The encore forced Goodman to make his only audience announcement for the night, stating that they had no encore prepared but that Martha would return shortly with another number. [13]

By the time the band got to the climactic piece "Sing, Sing, Sing," success of the night was assured. Bettering the commercial 12-inch record, this live performance featured playing by tenor saxophonist Babe Russin, trumpeter Harry James, and then Benny Goodman, backed by drummer Gene Krupa in accompaniment. But the really unforgettable moment came when Goodman finished his solo and unexpectedly tossed the ball to pianist Jess Stacy. "At the Carnegie Hall concert, after the usual theatrics, Jess Stacy was allowed to solo and, given the venue, what followed was appropriate. Used to just playing rhythm on the tune, he was unprepared for a turn in the spotlight, but what came out of his fingers was a graceful, impressionistic marvel with classical flourishes, yet still managed to swing. It was the best thing he ever did, and it's ironic that such a layered, nuanced performance came at the end of such a chaotic, bombastic tune."[14]

This concert has been regarded by some as the most significant in jazz history. After years of work by musicians from all over the country, jazz had finally been accepted by mainstream audiences. While the big band era would not last for much longer, it was from this point forward that the ground work for multiple other genres of popular music was laid.

Recordings were made of this concert, but even by the technology of the day the equipment used was not of the finest quality. Acetate recordings of the concert were made, and aluminum studio masters were also cut.

"The recording was produced by Albert Marx as a special gift for his wife, Helen Ward and a second set for Benny. He contracted Artists Recording Studio to make 2 sets. Artists Recording only had 2 turntables so they farmed out the second set to Raymond Scott's recording studio. [...] It was Benny's sister-in-law who found the recordings in Benny's apartment [in 1950] and brought them to Benny's attention."[15]

Goodman took the newly discovered recording to his record company, Columbia, and a selection from them was issued on LP. These recording have not been out of print since they were first issued.

In early 1998, the aluminum masters were rediscovered and a new CD set of the concert was released based on these masters.

Charlie Christian

Pianist/arranger Mary Lou Williams[8] was a good friend of Columbia records producer John Hammond's and Benny Goodman's. She first suggested to John Hammond that he see Charlie Christian.[9]

"Charlie Christian was playing at the Ritz Cafe in Oklahoma City where [...] John Hammond heard him in 1939. Hammond recommended him to Benny Goodman, but the band leader wasn't interested. The idea of an electrified guitar didn't appeal, and Goodman didn't care for Christian's flashy style of dressing. Reportedly, Hammond personally installed Christian onstage during reak in a Goodman concert in Beverly Hills. Irritated to see Christian among the band, Goodman struck up "Rose Room," not expecting the guitarist to know the tune. What followed amazed everyone who heard the 45-minute performance."[10]

"Charlie was a hit on the electric guitar and remained in the Benny Goodman Sextet for two years (1939-1941). He wrote many of the group's head arrangements (some of which Goodman took credit for) and was an inspiration to all. The sextet made him famous and provided him with a steady income while Charlie worked on legitimizing, popularizing, revolutionizing, and standardizing the electric guitar as a jazz instrument."[11]

Christian eventually stayed in New York City, jamming with bop musicians at Minton's in Harlem. "Charlie impressed them all by improvising long lines that emphasized off beats, and by using altered chords."[12] Charlie Christian died in Staten Island, March 2, 1942 of tuberculosis. Helping to broaden the form of jazz, Benny Goodman gave the nascent talent a huge start. Charlie Christian's recordings and rehearsal dubs he made at Columbia records with Benny Goodman in the early forties are widely known and widely respected.

Beyond Swing

Goodman continued his meteoric rise throughout
the late 1930s with his big band, his trio and
quartet, and a sextet. He influenced almost every
jazz musician who played clarinet after him.
However, in time the movement in jazz that he
ignited in 1935 began to fade. By the mid-1940s,
big bands lost a lot of their popularity. There were
several reasons for this decline. In 1941, ASCAP
had a licensing war with music publishers. In 1942
to 1944 and 1948, the major musicians union went
on strike against the major record labels in the
United States, and singers took the spot in
popularity that the big bands once enjoyed.[16]
Also, by the late 1940s, swing was no longer the
dominant mode of jazz musicians.[17]

Bebop, Cool Jazz

By the 1940s, jazz musicians were borrowing
some of the more advanced ideas that classical
musicians had been using. Bebop and then later
cool jazz were beginning to be heard. The
recordings Goodman made in the bop style for

Capitol Records were highly praised by jazz critics. When Goodman was starting ebop band, he hired Buddy Greco, Zoot Sims, Wardell Gray and a few other modern players.[18]

Pianist/arranger Mary Lou Williams had been a favorite of Benny's since she first appeared on the national scene in 1936 [...]. [A]s Goodman warily approached the music of [Charlie] Parker and [Dizzy] Gillespie, he turned to Williams for musical guidance. [...] Pianist Mel Powell was the first to introduce the new music to Benny in 1945, and kept him abreast to what was happening around 52nd Street.[18]

Goodman enjoyed the new music of bebop and cool jazz that was beginning to arrive in the nineteen forties. When Goodman heard Thelonious Monk, a celebrated pianist and accompanist to bop players Parker, Gillespie and Kenny Clarke, he remarked, "I like it, I like that very much. I like the piece and I like the way he played it. [...] I think he's got a sense of humor and he's got some good things there."[18]

'"Benny had heard this Swedish clarinet player named Stan Hasselgard playing bebop, and he loved it [...] [.]' 'So he started ebop band. But after a year and a half, he became frustrated. He eventually reformed his band and went back to playing Fletcher Henderson arrangements. Benny was a swing player and decided to concentrate on what he does best."[19]

By 1953, Goodman completely changed his mind about bebop. "Maybe bop has done more to set music back for years than anything [...] Basically it's all wrong. It's not even knowing the scales. [...] Bop was mostly publicity and people figuring angles."[20]

Forays into the Classical Repertoire

After his bop period, Goodman furthered his interest in classical music written for the clarinet, and frequently met with top classical clarinetists of the day as well.

In 1949, when he was 40, Goodman decided to study with Reginald Kell, one of the world's leading classical clarinetists. To do so, he had to change his entire technique: instead of holding the mouthpiece between his front teeth and lower lip, as he had done since he first took a clarinet in hand 30 years earlier, Goodman learned to adjust his embouchure to the use of both lips and even to use new fingering techniques. He had his old finger calluses removed and started to learn how to play his clarinet again--almost from scratch.[21]

Goodman commissioned and premiered works by leading composers for clarinet and symphony orchestra that are now part of the standard repertoire, namely Contrasts by Béla Bartók, Clarinet Concerto No. 2 Op. 115 by Malcolm Arnold and Aaron Copland's Clarinet Concerto. While Leonard Bernstein's Prelude, Fugue, and Riffs was commissioned for Woody Herman's big band, it was premiered by Goodman. While the Ebony Concerto by Igor Stravinsky is generally also thought to be written for Goodman, it was actually also written for Woody Herman in 1945, and premiered by him in 1946. "Many years later Stravinsky made another recording, this time with Benny Goodman as the soloist."[22] He twice recorded Mozart's clarinet quintet, once in the late 1930s with the Budapest String Quartet and once in the middle 1950s with the Boston Symphony Orchestra String Quartet; he also recorded the clarinet concertos of Wolfgang Amadeus Mozart, Carl Maria von Weber, and Carl Nielsen.[23]

Other recordings of classical repertoire by Goodman are[24]:

* Premiere Rhapsodie for Clarinet by Claude Debussy

* Sonata no. 2 in E flat by Johannes Brahms

* Rondo from Grand Duo Concertant in E flat from Carl Maria von Weber, and

* An arrangement by Simeon Bellison of van Beethoven's Variations on a theme from Mozart's Don Giovanni

Touring with "Satchmo"

After forays outside of swing, Goodman started a new band in 1953. According to Donald Clarke, this was not a happy time for Goodman.

In 1953 Goodman re-formed his classic band for an expensive tour with Louis Armstrong's All Stars that turned into a famous disaster. He managed to insult Armstrong at the beginning; then he was appalled at the vaudeville aspects of Louis's act [...] a contradiction of everything Goodman stood for.[25]

The Movies

Benny Goodman's band appeared as a specialty act in major musical features, including The Big Broadcast of 1937, Hollywood Hotel (1938), Syncopation (1942), The Powers Girl (1942), Stage Door Canteen (1943), The Gang's All Here (1943), Sweet and Lowdown (1944) and A Song Is Born (1948). Goodman's only starring feature was Sweet and Low Down (1944).

Goodman's success story was told in the 1955 motion picture The Benny Goodman Story[26] with Steve Allen and Donna Reed. A Universal-International production, it was a follow up to 1954's successful The Glenn Miller Story. The screenplay was heavily fictionalized (Benny confessed that he and his wife would look at the finished film and laugh through it), but the music was the real drawing card. Many of Goodman's professional colleagues appear in the film, including Ben Pollack. Gene Krupa, Lionel Hampton. and Harry James.

Personality and Influence on American Popular Music

Goodman was regarded by some as a demanding taskmaster, by others an arrogant and eccentric martinet. Many musicians spoke of "The Ray"[27] , Goodman's trademark glare that he bestowed on a musician who failed to perform to his demanding standards. Guitarist Allan Reuss incurred the maestro's displeasure on one occasion, and Goodman relegated him to the rear of the bandstand, where his contribution would be totally drowned out by the other musicians. Vocalists Anita O'Day and Helen Forrest spoke bitterly of their experiences singing with Goodman.[28] "The twenty or so months I spent with Benny felt like twenty years," said Forrest. "When I look back, they seem like a life sentence." He could also be incredibly self-absorbed; it is reported that when eating an egg onto which a ketchup bottle cap had fallen, Goodman simply ate around it.[11] At the same time, there are reports that he privately funded several college educations and was sometimes very generous, though always secretly. When a friend asked him why one time, he reportedly said, "Well, if they knew about it, everyone would come to me with their hand out."[28]

Some suggest that Elvis Presley had the same success with rock and roll that Goodman achieved with jazz and swing. Both helped bring black music to a young, white audience. Without Goodman there would not have been a swing era. It is true that many of Goodman's arrangements had been played for years before by Fletcher Henderson's orchestra. While Goodman publicly acknowledged his debt to Henderson, many young white swing fans had never heard Henderson's band. While most consider Goodman a jazz innovator, others maintain his main strength was his perfectionism and drive. Goodman was a virtuoso clarinetist and amongst the most technically proficient jazz clarinetists of all time.

Goodman is also responsible for a significant step in racial integration in America. In the early 1930s, black and white jazz musicians could not play together in most clubs or concerts. In the Southern states, racial segregation was enforced by the Jim Crow laws. Benny Goodman broke with tradition by hiring Teddy Wilson to play with him and drummer Gene Krupa in the Benny Goodman Trio. In 1936, he added Lionel Hampton on vibes to form the Benny Goodman Quartet; in 1939 he added pioneering jazz guitarist Charlie Christian to his band and small ensembles, who played with him until his untimely death from tuberculosis less than three years later. To give an understanding of American history at this time, Goodman's integration of popular music happened ten years before Jackie Robinson became the first black American to enter Major League Baseball. "[Goodman's] popularity was such that he could remain financially viable without touring the South, where he would have been subject to arrest for violating Jim Crow laws."[30] According to Jazz by Ken Burns, when someone asked him why he "played with that nigger" (referring to Teddy Wilson), Goodman replied, "I'll knock you out if you use that word around me again".

John Hammond and Alice Goodman

One of Benny Goodman's closest friends off and on, from the 1930s onward was celebrated Columbia records producer John H. Hammond.

John Henry Hammond II was born December 15, 1910 in an eight-story mansion in New York City. He was the son of James Henry Hammond, a very successful businessman and lawyer, and Emily Vanderbilt Sloane, an heir to the Sloan Furniture and - as a granddaughter of William Henry Vanderbilt - to the Vanderbilt fortunes. John H. Hammond II attended the esteemed Hotchkiss Prep School and Yale University.[31]

Hammond and Goodman were so close that Hammond influenced Goodman's move from RCA records to the newly created Columbia records in 1939.[32] Benny Goodman dated John H. Hammond's sister, Alice Frances Hammond (? - 1978) for three months. They married on March 14, 1942. They had two daughters, Benjie and Rachel.[33] Both daughters studied music to some degree, though neither became the musical prodigy Goodman was. Hammond had encouraged Goodman to integrate his band, having persuaded him to employ pianist Teddy Wilson. He all but forced Goodman to audition Charlie Christian, Goodman believing no one would listen to an electric guitarist. But Hammond's tendency to interfere in the musical affairs of Goodman's and other bands led to Goodman pulling away from him. In 1953 they had another falling-out during Goodman's ill-fated tour with Louis Armstrong, which was produced by John Hammond.[34] Goodman appeared on a 1975 PBS salute to Hammond but remained at a distance. In the 1980s, following the death of Alice Goodman, John Hammond and Benny Goodman, both by then elderly, reconciled. On June 25, 1985, Goodman appeared at Avery Fisher Hall in New York City for "A Tribute to John Hammond".[35]

Later Years

Goodman continued to play on records and in small groups. One exception to this pattern was a collaboration with George Benson in the 1970s. The two had met when they taped a PBS salute to John Hammond and re-created some of the

famous Goodman-Charlie Christian duets.[36]
Benson later appeared on several tracks of a
Goodman album released as "Seven Come
Eleven." In general Goodman continued to play in
the swing style he was most known for. He did,
however, practice and perform classical music
clarinet pieces and commissioned some pieces for
the clarinet. Periodically he would organize a new
band and play a jazz festival or go on an
international tour.

Despite increasing health problems, he continued
to play the clarinet until his death from a heart
attack in New York City in 1986 at the age of 77.
A longtime resident of Pound Ridge, New York,
Benny Goodman is interred in the Long Ridge
Cemetery, Stamford, Connecticut. The same year,
Goodman was honored with the Grammy Lifetime
Achievement Award.[37] Benny Goodman's
musical papers were donated to Yale University
after his death.[4]

Discography

(This discography combines LP and CD reissues of Goodman recordings under the dates of the original 78 rpm recordings through about 1950)

* A Jazz Holiday (1928, Decca)

* Benny Goodman and the Giants of Swing (1929, Prestige)

* BG and Big Tea in NYC (1929, GRP)

* Swinging '34 Vols. 1 & 2 (1934, Melodean)

* Sing, Sing, Sing (1935, Bluebird)

* The Birth of Swing (1935, Bluebird)

* Original Benny Goodman Trio and Quartet Sessions, Vol. 1: After You've Gone (1935, Bluebird)

* Stomping at the Savoy (1935, Bluebird)

* Air Play (1936, Doctor Jazz)

* Roll 'Em, Vol. 1 (1937, Columbia)

* Roll 'Em, Vol. 2 (1937, CBS)

* From Spirituals to Swing (1938, Vanguard)

* Carnegie Hall Jazz Concert (1938, Columbia)

* Carnegie Hall Concert Vols. 1, 2, & 3 (Live) (1938, Columbia)

* Ciribiribin (Live) (1939, Giants of Jazz)

* Swingin' Down the Lane (Live) (1939, Giants of Jazz)

* Featuring Charlie Christian (1939, Columbia)

* Eddie Sauter Arrangements (1940, Columbia)

* Swing Into Spring (1941, Columbia)

* Undercurrent Blues (1947, Blue Note)

* Swedish Pastry (1948, Dragon)

* Sextet (1950, Columbia)

* BG in Hi-fi (1954, Capitol)

* Peggy Lee Sings with Benny Goodman (1957, Harmony)

* Benny in Brussels Vols. 1 & 2 (1958, Columbia)

* In Stockholm 1959 (1959, Phontastic)

* The Benny Goodman Treasure Chest (1959, MGM)

* The King Swings Star Line

* Pure Gold (1992)

* 1935-1938 (1998)

* Portrait of Benny Goodman (Portrait Series) (1998)

* Carnegie Hall Jazz Concert '38 (1998)

* Bill Dodge All-star Recording (1999)

* 1941-1955 His Orchestra and His (1999)

* Live at Carnegie Hall (1999)

* Carnegie Hall: The Complete Concert (2006) Remastered again

Samples

* of "And the Angels Sing" by Benny Goodman and Martha Tilton, a legendary swing recording that helped keep Goodman's career afloat as the band members departed.

The King of Swing

References

1. Firestone, Ross (1993). Swing, Swing, Swing: The Life and Times of Benny Goodman. New York: Norton, pp. 19.

2. The days

3. Firestone, Ross (1993). Swing, Swing, Swing: The Life and Times of Benny Goodman. New York: Norton, pp. 18.

4. JAZZ A Film By Ken Burns: Selected Artist Biography - Benny Goodman. PBS (2001-01-08). Retrieved on 2007-03-29.

5. Firestone, Ross (1993). Swing, Swing, Swing: The Life and Times of Benny Goodman. New York: Norton, pp. 26-34.

6. Firestone, Ross (1993). Swing, Swing, Swing: The Life and Times of Benny Goodman. New York: Norton, pp. 35.

7. Collier, James Lincoln (1989). Benny Goodman and the Swing Era. Oxford University Press.

8. Firestone, Ross (1993). Swing, Swing, Swing: The Life and Times of Benny Goodman. New York: Norton, pp. 42.

9. 70 Years Ago: Goodman Opens at the Palomar (2005-08-20). Retrieved on 2007-03-29.

10. BBC (2006-03-22). Jitterbug. Retrieved on 2007-03-29.

11. Will Friedwald (2006-11-20). Arts and Letters: Peplowski Blows Back to His Roots. Retrieved on 2007-03-29.

12. Mike Joyce. The 1938 Carnegie Hall Concert. Retrieved on 2007-03-29.

13. "insert booklet", "The Famous 1938 Carnegie Hall Jazz Concert" Sony 199 2 CD reissue .

14. David Rickert (2005-01-31). Benny Goodman: "Sing, Sing, Sing". Retrieved on 2007-03-29.

15. Firestone, Ross (1993). Swing, Swing, Swing: The Life and Times of Benny Goodman. New York: Norton, pp. 366.

16. http://www.swingmusic.net/Big_Band_Era_Recor ding_Ban_Of_1942.html

17. http://www.allaboutjazz.com/timeline.htm

18. Schoenberg, Loren (1995), "Liner Notes", Benny Goodman: Undercurrent Blues

19. http://www.post-gazette.com/pg/05128/499780.stm

20. Firestone, Ross (1993). Swing, Swing, Swing: The Life and Times of Benny Goodman. New York: Norton, pp. 354.

21. http://cms.westport.k12.ct.us/cmslmc/music/jazzbi os/goodman.htm

22. http://www.compactdiscoveries.com/CompactDisc overiesArticles/Yeh.html

23. Firestone, Ross (1993). Swing, Swing, Swing: The Life and Times of Benny Goodman. New York: Norton, pp. 246-247, 250, 252, 324.

24. Available on compact disc: Benny Goodman - Clarinet Classics, Pavilion Records Ltd. Pearl GEM0057

25. Donald Clarke. The Rise and Fall of Popular Music. Retrieved on 2007-02-30.

26. http://www.imdb.com/title/tt0047873/

27. Firestone, Ross (1993). Swing, Swing, Swing: The Life and Times of Benny Goodman. New York: Norton, p. 173.

28. Firestone, Ross (1993). Swing, Swing, Swing: The Life and Times of Benny Goodman. New York: Norton, pp. 296, 301-302, 401.

29. "Ibid"; Firestone, Ross p. 183-184.

30. http://www.nndb.com/people/755/000026677/

31. Charlie Dahan. Jazz Impressario: John Hammond. Retrieved on 2007-03-30.

32. Firestone, Ross (1993). Swing, Swing, Swing: The Life and Times of Benny Goodman. New York: Norton, pp. 258-259.

33. Firestone, Ross (1993). Swing, Swing, Swing: The Life and Times of Benny Goodman. New York: Norton, pp. 309-310.

34. Firestone, Ross (1993). Swing, Swing, Swing: The Life and Times of Benny Goodman. New York: Norton, pp. 380.

35. John S. Wilson (1985-06-29). JAZZ FESTIVAL; BENNY GOODMAN JOINS JOHN HAMMOND TRIBUTE. New York Times. Retrieved on 2007-04-02.

36. Firestone, Ross (1993). Swing, Swing, Swing: The Life and Times of Benny Goodman. New York: Norton, pp. 433-434.

37. Lifetime Achievement Award. The Recording Academy. Retrieved on 2007-04-02.

Benny Goodman

GNU Free Documentation License

Version 1.2, November 2002

0. PREAMBLE

The purpose of this License is to make a manual, textbook, or other
functional and useful document "free" in the sense of freedom: to assure
everyone the effective freedom to copy and redistribute it, with or without
modifying it, either commercially or noncommercially. Secondarily, this
License preserves for the author and publisher a way to get credit for their
work, while not being considered responsible for modifications made by
others.

This License is a kind of "copyleft", which means that derivative works of
the document must themselves be free in the same sense. It complements
the GNU General Public License, which is a copyleft license designed for
free software.

We have designed this License in order to use it for manuals for free
software, because free software needs free documentation: a free program
should come with manuals providing the same freedoms that the software
does. But this License is not limited to software manuals; it can be used for
any textual work, regardless of subject matter or whether it is published as a
printed book. We recommend this License principally for works whose
purpose is instruction or reference.

The King of Swing

1. APPLICABILITY AND DEFINITIONS

This License applies to any manual or other work, in any medium, that contains a notice placed by the copyright holder saying it can be distributed under the terms of this License. Such a notice grants a world-wide, royalty-free license, unlimited in duration, to use that work under the conditions stated herein. The "Document", below, refers to any such manual or work. Any member of the public is a licensee, and is addressed as "you". You accept the license if you copy, modify or distribute the work in a way requiring permission under copyright law.

A "Modified Version" of the Document means any work containing the Document or a portion of it, either copied verbatim, or with modifications and/or translated into another language.

A "Secondary Section" is a named appendix or a front-matter section of the Document that deals exclusively with the relationship of the publishers or authors of the Document to the Document's overall subject (or to related matters) and contains nothing that could fall directly within that overall subject. (Thus, if the Document is in part a textbook of mathematics, a Secondary Section may not explain any mathematics.) The relationship could be a matter of historical connection with the subject or with related matters, or of legal, commercial, philosophical, ethical or political position regarding them.

The "Invariant Sections" are certain Secondary Sections whose titles are designated, as being those of Invariant Sections, in the notice that says that the Document is released under this License. If a section does not fit the above definition of Secondary then it is not allowed to be designated as Invariant. The Document may contain zero Invariant Sections. If the Document does not identify any Invariant Sections then there are none.

The "Cover Texts" are certain short passages of text that are listed, as Front-Cover Texts or Back-Cover Texts, in the notice that says that the Document is released under this License. A Front-Cover Text may be at most 5 words, and a Back-Cover Text may be at most 25 words.

Benny Goodman

A "Transparent" copy of the Document means a machine-readable copy, represented in a format whose specification is available to the general public, that is suitable for revising the document straightforwardly with generic text editors or (for images composed of pixels) generic paint programs or (for drawings) some widely available drawing editor, and that is suitable for input to text formatters or for automatic translation to a variety of formats suitable for input to text formatters. A copy made in an otherwise Transparent file format whose markup, or absence of markup, has been arranged to thwart or discourage subsequent modification by readers is not Transparent. An image format is not Transparent if used for any substantial amount of text. A copy that is not "Transparent" is called "Opaque".

Examples of suitable formats for Transparent copies include plain ASCII without markup, Texinfo input format, LaTeX input format, SGML or XML using a publicly available DTD, and standard-conforming simple HTML, PostScript or PDF designed for human modification. Examples of transparent image formats include PNG, XCF and JPG. Opaque formats include proprietary formats that can be read and edited only by proprietary word processors, SGML or XML for which the DTD and/or processing tools are not generally available, and the machine-generated HTML, PostScript or PDF produced by some word processors for output purposes only.

The "Title Page" means, for a printed book, the title page itself, plus such following pages as are needed to hold, legibly, the material this License requires to appear in the title page. For works in formats which do not have any title page as such, "Title Page" means the text near the most prominent appearance of the work's title, preceding the beginning of the body of the text.

A section "Entitled XYZ" means a named subunit of the Document whose title either is precisely XYZ or contains XYZ in parentheses following text that translates XYZ in another language. (Here XYZ stands for a specific section name mentioned below, such as "Acknowledgements", "Dedications", "Endorsements", or "History".) To "Preserve the Title" of such a section when you modify the Document means that it remains a section "Entitled XYZ" according to this definition.

The King of Swing

The Document may include Warranty Disclaimers next to the notice which states that this License applies to the Document. These Warranty Disclaimers are considered to be included by reference in this License, but only as regards disclaiming warranties: any other implication that these Warranty Disclaimers may have is void and has no effect on the meaning of this License.

2. VERBATIM COPYING

You may copy and distribute the Document in any medium, either commercially or noncommercially, provided that this License, the copyright notices, and the license notice saying this License applies to the Document are reproduced in all copies, and that you add no other conditions whatsoever to those of this License. You may not use technical measures to obstruct or control the reading or further copying of the copies you make or distribute. However, you may accept compensation in exchange for copies. If you distribute a large enough number of copies you must also follow the conditions in section 3.

You may also lend copies, under the same conditions stated above, and you may publicly display copies.

3. COPYING IN QUANTITY

If you publish printed copies (or copies in media that commonly have printed covers) of the Document, numbering more than 100, and the Document's license notice requires Cover Texts, you must enclose the copies in covers that carry, clearly and legibly, all these Cover Texts: Front-Cover Texts on the front cover, and Back-Cover Texts on the back cover. Both covers must also clearly and legibly identify you as the publisher of these copies. The front cover must present the full title with all words of the title equally prominent and visible. You may add other material on the covers in addition. Copying with changes limited to the covers, as long as they preserve the title of the Document and satisfy these conditions, can be treated as verbatim copying in other respects.

If the required texts for either cover are too voluminous to fit legibly, you should put the first ones listed (as many as fit reasonably) on the actual cover, and continue the rest onto adjacent pages.

Benny Goodman

If you publish or distribute Opaque copies of the Document numbering more than 100, you must either include a machine-readable Transparent copy along with each Opaque copy, or state in or with each Opaque copy a computer-network location from which the general network-using public has access to download using public-standard network protocols a complete Transparent copy of the Document, free of added material. If you use the latter option, you must take reasonably prudent steps, when you begin distribution of Opaque copies in quantity, to ensure that this Transparent copy will remain thus accessible at the stated location until at least one year after the last time you distribute an Opaque copy (directly or through your agents or retailers) of that edition to the public.

It is requested, but not required, that you contact the authors of the Document well before redistributing any large number of copies, to give them a chance to provide you with an updated version of the Document.

4. MODIFICATIONS

You may copy and distribute a Modified Version of the Document under the conditions of sections 2 and 3 above, provided that you release the Modified Version under precisely this License, with the Modified Version filling the role of the Document, thus licensing distribution and modification of the Modified Version to whoever possesses a copy of it. In addition, you must do these things in the Modified Version:

* A. Use in the Title Page (and on the covers, if any) a title distinct from that of the Document, and from those of previous versions (which should, if there were any, be listed in the History section of the Document). You may use the same title as a previous version if the original publisher of that version gives permission.
* B. List on the Title Page, as authors, one or more persons or entities responsible for authorship of the modifications in the Modified Version, together with at least five of the principal authors of the Document (all of its principal authors, if it has fewer than five), unless they release you from this requirement.
* C. State on the Title page the name of the publisher of the Modified Version, as the publisher.
* D. Preserve all the copyright notices of the Document.

 * E. Add an appropriate copyright notice for your modifications adjacent to the other copyright notices.
 * F. Include, immediately after the copyright notices, a license notice giving the public permission to use the Modified Version under the terms of this License, in the form shown in the Addendum below.
 * G. Preserve in that license notice the full lists of Invariant Sections and required Cover Texts given in the Document's license notice.
 * H. Include an unaltered copy of this License.
 * I. Preserve the section Entitled "History", Preserve its Title, and add to it an item stating at least the title, year, new authors, and publisher of the Modified Version as given on the Title Page. If there is no section Entitled "History" in the Document, create one stating the title, year, authors, and publisher of the Document as given on its Title Page, then add an item describing the Modified Version as stated in the previous sentence.
 * J. Preserve the network location, if any, given in the Document for public access to a Transparent copy of the Document, and likewise the network locations given in the Document for previous versions it was based on. These may be placed in the "History" section. You may omit a network location for a work that was published at least four years before the Document itself, or if the original publisher of the version it refers to gives permission.
 * K. For any section Entitled "Acknowledgements" or "Dedications", Preserve the Title of the section, and preserve in the section all the substance and tone of each of the contributor acknowledgements and/or dedications given therein.
 * L. Preserve all the Invariant Sections of the Document, unaltered in their text and in their titles. Section numbers or the equivalent are not considered part of the section titles.
 * M. Delete any section Entitled "Endorsements". Such a section may not be included in the Modified Version.
 * N. Do not retitle any existing section to be Entitled "Endorsements" or to conflict in title with any Invariant Section.
 * O. Preserve any Warranty Disclaimers.

If the Modified Version includes new front-matter sections or appendices that qualify as Secondary Sections and contain no material copied from the Document, you may at your option designate some or all of these sections as invariant. To do this, add their titles to the list of Invariant Sections in the

Benny Goodman

Modified Version's license notice. These titles must be distinct from any other section titles.

You may add a section Entitled "Endorsements", provided it contains nothing but endorsements of your Modified Version by various parties--for example, statements of peer review or that the text has been approved by an organization as the authoritative definition of a standard.

You may add a passage of up to five words as a Front-Cover Text, and a passage of up to 25 words as a Back-Cover Text, to the end of the list of Cover Texts in the Modified Version. Only one passage of Front-Cover Text and one of Back-Cover Text may be added by (or through arrangements made by) any one entity. If the Document already includes a cover text for the same cover, previously added by you or by arrangement made by the same entity you are acting on behalf of, you may not add another; but you may replace the old one, on explicit permission from the previous publisher that added the old one.

The author(s) and publisher(s) of the Document do not by this License give permission to use their names for publicity for or to assert or imply endorsement of any Modified Version.

5. COMBINING DOCUMENTS

You may combine the Document with other documents released under this License, under the terms defined in section 4 above for modified versions, provided that you include in the combination all of the Invariant Sections of all of the original documents, unmodified, and list them all as Invariant Sections of your combined work in its license notice, and that you preserve all their Warranty Disclaimers.

The combined work need only contain one copy of this License, and multiple identical Invariant Sections may be replaced with a single copy. If there are multiple Invariant Sections with the same name but different contents, make the title of each such section unique by adding at the end of it, in parentheses, the name of the original author or publisher of that section if known, or else a unique number. Make the same adjustment to the section titles in the list of Invariant Sections in the license notice of the combined work.

In the combination, you must combine any sections Entitled "History" in the various original documents, forming one section Entitled "History"; likewise combine any sections Entitled "Acknowledgements", and any sections Entitled "Dedications". You must delete all sections Entitled "Endorsements."

6. COLLECTIONS OF DOCUMENTS

You may make a collection consisting of the Document and other documents released under this License, and replace the individual copies of this License in the various documents with a single copy that is included in the collection, provided that you follow the rules of this License for verbatim copying of each of the documents in all other respects.

You may extract a single document from such a collection, and distribute it individually under this License, provided you insert a copy of this License into the extracted document, and follow this License in all other respects regarding verbatim copying of that document.

7. AGGREGATION WITH INDEPENDENT WORKS

A compilation of the Document or its derivatives with other separate and independent documents or works, in or on a volume of a storage or distribution medium, is called an "aggregate" if the copyright resulting from the compilation is not used to limit the legal rights of the compilation's users beyond what the individual works permit. When the Document is included in an aggregate, this License does not apply to the other works in the aggregate which are not themselves derivative works of the Document.

If the Cover Text requirement of section 3 is applicable to these copies of the Document, then if the Document is less than one half of the entire aggregate, the Document's Cover Texts may be placed on covers that bracket the Document within the aggregate, or the electronic equivalent of covers if the Document is in electronic form. Otherwise they must appear on printed covers that bracket the whole aggregate.

8. TRANSLATION

Translation is considered a kind of modification, so you may distribute translations of the Document under the terms of section 4. Replacing Invariant Sections with translations requires special permission from their copyright holders, but you may include translations of some or all Invariant Sections in addition to the original versions of these Invariant Sections. You may include a translation of this License, and all the license notices in the Document, and any Warranty Disclaimers, provided that you also include the original English version of this License and the original versions of those notices and disclaimers. In case of a disagreement between the translation and the original version of this License or a notice or disclaimer, the original version will prevail.

If a section in the Document is Entitled "Acknowledgements", "Dedications", or "History", the requirement (section 4) to Preserve its Title (section 1) will typically require changing the actual title.

9. TERMINATION

You may not copy, modify, sublicense, or distribute the Document except as expressly provided for under this License. Any other attempt to copy, modify, sublicense or distribute the Document is void, and will automatically terminate your rights under this License. However, parties who have received copies, or rights, from you under this License will not have their licenses terminated so long as such parties remain in full compliance.

10. FUTURE REVISIONS OF THIS LICENSE

The Free Software Foundation may publish new, revised versions of the GNU Free Documentation License from time to time. Such new versions will be similar in spirit to the present version, but may differ in detail to address new problems or concerns. See http://www.gnu.org/copyleft/.

Each version of the License is given a distinguishing version number. If the Document specifies that a particular numbered version of this License "or any later version" applies to it, you have the option of following the terms and conditions either of that specified version or of any later version that has been published (not as a draft) by the Free Software Foundation. If the Document does not specify a version number of this License, you may choose any version ever published (not as a draft) by the Free Software Foundation.

How to use this License for your documents

To use this License in a document you have written, include a copy of the License in the document and put the following copyright and license notices just after the title page:

Copyright (c) YEAR YOUR NAME.
Permission is granted to copy, distribute and/or modify this document under the terms of the GNU Free Documentation License, Version 1.2 or any later version published by the Free Software Foundation; with no Invariant Sections, no Front-Cover Texts, and no Back-Cover Texts. A copy of the license is included in the section entitled "GNU
Free Documentation License".

If you have Invariant Sections, Front-Cover Texts and Back-Cover Texts, replace the "with...Texts." line with this:

with the Invariant Sections being LIST THEIR TITLES, with the Front-Cover Texts being LIST, and with the Back-Cover Texts being LIST.

If you have Invariant Sections without Cover Texts, or some other combination of the three, merge those two alternatives to suit the situation.

If your document contains nontrivial examples of program code, we recommend releasing these examples in parallel under your choice of free software license, such as the GNU General Public License, to permit their use in free software.

Printed in the United States
150663LV00008B/90/P